Published by Angelis Publications
ISBN: 978-0-9956949-3-4
www.angelispublications.com
Cover photo © Angie J Anderson
© Angelis Publications 2017

A Celebration of the Life of

"That we once enjoyed and deeply loved we can never lose, for all that we love deeply becomes part of us."

Helen Keller

Name & Address

Thoughts & Memories

Name & Address

Thoughts & Memories

Name & Address

Thoughts & Memories

Name & Address

Thoughts & Memories

Name & Address

Thoughts & Memories

Name & Address

Thoughts & Memories

Name & Address

Thoughts & Memories

Name & Address

Thoughts & Memories

Name & Address

Thoughts & Memories

Name & Address

Thoughts & Memories

Name & Address

Thoughts & Memories

Name & Address

Thoughts & Memories

Name & Address

Thoughts & Memories

Name & Address

Thoughts & Memories

Name & Address

Thoughts & Memories

Name & Address

Thoughts & Memories

Name & Address

Thoughts & Memories

Name & Address

Thoughts & Memories

Name & Address

Thoughts & Memories

Name & Address   Thoughts & Memories

Name & Address

Thoughts & Memories

Name & Address

Thoughts & Memories

Name & Address

Thoughts & Memories

Name & Address

Thoughts & Memories

Name & Address

Thoughts & Memories

Name & Address

Thoughts & Memories

Name & Address

_____

_____

_____

_____

_____

_____

_____

_____

_____

_____

_____

_____

_____

Thoughts & Memories

_____

_____

_____

_____

_____

_____

_____

_____

_____

_____

_____

_____

_____

Name & Address

Thoughts & Memories

Name & Address

Thoughts & Memories

Name & Address

Thoughts & Memories

Name & Address

Thoughts & Memories

Name & Address

Thoughts & Memories

Name & Address

Thoughts & Memories

Name & Address

Thoughts & Memories

Name & Address

Thoughts & Memories

Name & Address

Thoughts & Memories

Name & Address

Thoughts & Memories

Name & Address

Thoughts & Memories

Name & Address

Thoughts & Memories

Name & Address

Thoughts & Memories

Name & Address

Thoughts & Memories

Name & Address

Thoughts & Memories

Name & Address

Thoughts & Memories

Name & Address

Thoughts & Memories

Name & Address

Thoughts & Memories

Name & Address

Thoughts & Memories

Name & Address

Thoughts & Memories

Name & Address

Thoughts & Memories

Name & Address

Thoughts & Memories

Name & Address

Thoughts & Memories

Name & Address

Thoughts & Memories

Name & Address

Thoughts & Memories

Name & Address

Thoughts & Memories

Name & Address

Thoughts & Memories

Name & Address

Thoughts & Memories

Name & Address

Thoughts & Memories

Name & Address

Thoughts & Memories

Name & Address

Thoughts & Memories

Name & Address

Thoughts & Memories

Name & Address

Thoughts & Memories

Name & Address

Thoughts & Memories

Name & Address

Thoughts & Memories

Name & Address

Thoughts & Memories

Name & Address

Thoughts & Memories

Name & Address

Thoughts & Memories

Name & Address

Thoughts & Memories

Name & Address

Thoughts & Memories

Name & Address

Thoughts & Memories

Name & Address

Thoughts & Memories

Name & Address

Thoughts & Memories

Name & Address

Thoughts & Memories

Name & Address

Thoughts & Memories

Name & Address

Thoughts & Memories

Name & Address

Thoughts & Memories

Name & Address

Thoughts & Memories

Name & Address　　　*Thoughts & Memories*

Name & Address

Thoughts & Memories

Name & Address

Thoughts & Memories

Name & Address

Thoughts & Memories

Name & Address

Thoughts & Memories

Name & Address

Thoughts & Memories

Name & Address

Thoughts & Memories

Name & Address

Thoughts & Memories

Name & Address

Thoughts & Memories

Name & Address

Thoughts & Memories

Name & Address

Thoughts & Memories

Name & Address

Thoughts & Memories

Name & Address

Thoughts & Memories

Name & Address

Thoughts & Memories

Name & Address

Thoughts & Memories

Name & Address

Thoughts & Memories

Name & Address

Thoughts & Memories

Name & Address

Thoughts & Memories

Name & Address

Thoughts & Memories

CPSIA information can be obtained
at www.ICGtesting.com
Printed in the USA
LVHW060718210723
752968LV00019B/67